FOOTBALL

Ted Cox

RIGBY
INTERACTIVE
LIBRARY

This edition © 1997 Rigby Education
Published by Rigby Interactive Library,
an imprint of Rigby Education,
division of Reed Elsevier, Inc.
500 Coventry Lane
Crystal Lake, IL 60014

Printed in the United States of America

00 99 98 97 96
10 9 8 7 6 5 4 3 2 1

Library of Congress Cataloging-in-Publication Data
Cox, Ted.
     Football / by Ted Cox.
          p.   cm. — (Successful sports)
     Includes index.
     Summary: Surveys the attitudes, skills, equipment, and tactics
involved in playing football well.
     ISBN 1-57572-067-1
     1. Football—Juvenile literature. [1. Football.] I. Title. II. Series.
GV950.7.C69 1996
796.332—dc20
                                                              96-7514
                                                                 CIP
                                                                  AC

Acknowledgments
The publishers would like to thank the following for permission
to reproduce photographs:

Allsport USA/Jamie Squire: p. 20; Allsport USA/Jonathan
Daniel: pp. 2, 7; Allsport USA/Pete J. Groh: p. 28;
Allsport USA/Stephen Dunn: p. 11; AP/Wide World
Photos: pp. 18, 22; AP/Wide World Photos/Dallas
Morning News/Phil Huber: p. 5; AP/Wide World
Photos/Mark Elias: p. 10; AP/Wide World
Photos/Eric Gay: p. 24; Duomo/William R.
Sallaz: p.18; Focus on Sports: p. 26; David
Madison: pp. 12, 28; John Morrison: copyright
page, p. 21; PhotoEdit/©Tony Freeman: pp.
16, 17; Sean Ryan Photography: pp. 4, 27;
Sports Photo Masters/© Don Smith: pp. 8,
15; Sports Photo Masters/©Mitchell
Reibel: p. 9; Sports Photo Masters/
©Marc Levine: front cover;

Illustrator:
Stephen Brayfield: pp. 6, 9, 15, 17, 25.

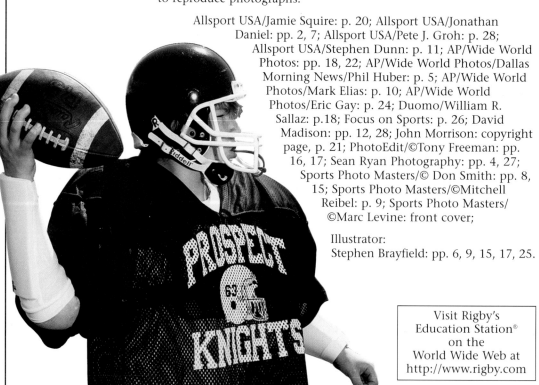

Contents

The Fastest-Growing Sport

American football is one of the quickest, most exciting, and fastest-growing sports in the world. From its simple origins developing from the game of Rugby at American universities in the mid-1800s, football has become a worldwide sensation. Professional teams play football for a living in big cities, and amateurs play at colleges and high schools. Wherever people gather in the fall and winter—football season—they can be seen tossing around "the old **pigskin**" in back yards, playgrounds, and even city streets.

That's right: tossing as well as kicking. Unlike soccer, which the rest of the world calls "football," American football is played with the feet as well as the hands. As in Rugby, the main object is to carry the ball across a goal line. But, unlike Rugby, football allows the forward **pass** as well as the backward lateral. What's more, the ball can be kicked through a set of **goal posts** for points as well, and a team can surrender the ball and push the other team back by **punting** it away. So, the feet do have something to do with it after all!

Football's popularity has spread overseas. This photograph shows an amateur game between the London Olympians and the Birmingham Bulls.

It might all sound complicated at first, but it isn't really. The basics of football are easy to understand. While football rules are always somewhat in flux, the basics remain pretty much the same.

The size of a football field can vary. It could be almost any size, and the game would still be football. But the football itself, that is something unique to the sport. It is round but also oval, pointed but with no sharp edges. Its shape is called a prolate spheroid, a three-dimensional circle drawn out at opposite ends. In the early days of football, the ball was more round, more like a soccer or Rugby ball. But as the game's pace quickened and more emphasis was put on passing, the ball was made thinner, better able to fly through the air, and easier to handle. By that time, the regulation football field was set.

FOOTBALL FACTS

The NFL plays a 60-minute game, which is divided into four 15-minute quarters and two halves, split by a half-time intermission. American colleges play four 12-minute quarters, and high schools usually play four 8-minute quarters.

Dwight Clark stretches out to make a game-winning catch for the San Francisco 49ers in the 1981 NFL Championship game.

Gridiron Guide

The football field is commonly called the *gridiron*, because it is laid out in a rectangular grid pattern. The regulation U.S. football field is 120 yards long and 53⅓ yards wide. There is nothing mysterious or magical about the field's width. The regulation football field is 53⅓ yards wide because, when Yale University's football coach Walter Camp was trying to establish the standard size in the late 1800s, that was the widest field that could fit inside the stadium of rival Harvard University.

There is something magical, however, about the length of the field from **end zone** to end zone: an even 100 yards. The two end zones are 10 yards deep to allow players to maneuver there without being ruled out of bounds. At the back of the end zones are goal posts—18½ feet apart and with a crossbar 10 feet off the ground—for points scored by kicking.

PRO HASH MARKS

COLLEGE HASH MARKS

The gridiron, or football field.

Usually, lines are drawn across the width of the field every five yards. These lines are numbered every 10 yards from end zone to midfield, which is called the 50-yard line. The numbers count up from both end zones to midfield, to signify that each team has a goal to defend. When a team marches the ball downfield from near its own goal line, it counts up to midfield and then down to the other team's goal.

At the middle of the field are **hash marks**. When a player runs out of bounds with the ball, it is ruled down on the spot, and the next play starts at the nearest hash mark. In the **National Football League (NFL)**, the hash marks are 18½ feet apart—the same width as the goal posts. In college football, the hash marks are 23⅓ feet apart. This has helped put more emphasis on speed in college, because of the wide expanse of field from a hashmark to the far **sideline.**

Moving the Ball

The game begins with one team kicking the ball to the other team off a tee near the ground, starting at the kicking team's 35-yard or 40-yard line. The kicking team usually is picked by a coin flip. The receiving team gets a chance to return the **kickoff** and then begins a set of plays, or downs.

Possession of the ball dictates which team of eleven players is on offense and which team is on defense. The ball can be carried forward, and a player can pass the ball backward to a teammate, a play known as a *lateral*.

Unlike Rugby, football allows the forward pass. That is, the ball may be thrown forward from behind the **line of scrimmage**, where the play began, to a receiver down the field. If the pass falls to the ground without being caught, the ball returns to the original spot at the beginning of the play.

Jerry Rice lunges for a first down.

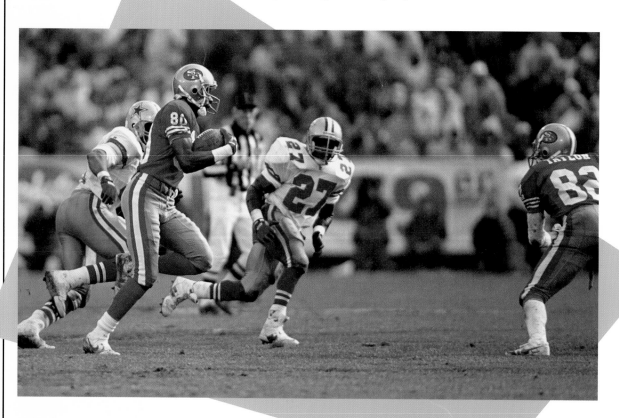

FOOTBALL FACTS

The defensive team can intercept the pass, thus claiming possession of the ball. Whenever a player drops the ball to the ground before he is **tackled** or ruled down, that is a **fumble.** The ball is up for grabs! Whichever teams gets it first runs the next offensive play.

The offensive team must advance the ball to keep it. A team has four downs to move the ball ten yards. If it fails, the ball goes to the other team. Whenever a team moves ahead ten yards from the first-down spot, a new set of downs begins.

A team may decide, however, that there is too much ground to be gained to make the effort worthwhile. Especially if a team is in its own territory, short of the 50-yard line, it may surrender the ball by punting on fourth down. The punter stands about 15 yards behind the line of scrimmage. When the play begins with the **hike** from center, he drops it in front of him and kicks it away before it touches the ground. The receiving team then gets a chance to return the punt before beginning a new set of downs.

Girls play at the high school level. This player kicks a field goal.

Pointers

A team can punt the ball away on any down. Sometimes, a team stuck near its own end zone might decide to have the quarterback or a running back punt the ball away by surprise on second or third down, a tactic known as a quick kick.

Scoring

The object of play is simple: to get the ball in the end zone. In football's early days, a runner who reached the end zone would touch the ball to the ground to show a score. Today, this type of score still is called a **touchdown**. But players no longer have to touch the ball to the ground. They must simply carry the ball across the plane of the end zone, the imaginary wall that extends straight up from the goal line, or catch the ball inside the end zone. Either way, it's six points.

After the touchdown, the scoring team gets a chance to kick an **extra point**. The ball is placed on the 3-yard line. The ball is hiked to a holder, who is usually seven yards back at the 10-yard line. The kicker tries to kick the ball through the uprights for a successful point after touchdown (PAT). In college and NFL football, the scoring team may choose to run an offensive play from the 3-yard line. This strategy is more difficult than a PAT, so that play is worth two points and is known as the two-point conversion.

Walter Payton dives into the end zone to score a touchdown.

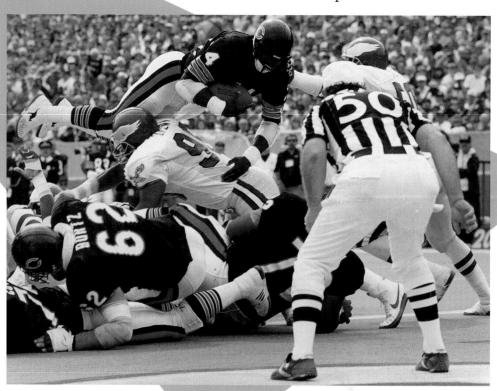

Teams that fail to reach the end zone can opt to kick a **field goal**, usually on fourth down when they have too far to go to reach either a first down or the end zone. Field goals can be tried from anywhere on the field. Again, the holder awaits the hike about seven yards behind the line of scrimmage. The kicker tries to boot the ball through the uprights for a field goal, which is worth three points.

Defensive players can score by returning an **interception** or a fumble to the end zone. The defense can also score by tackling the offensive ball carrier inside his own end zone— a play known as a **safety.** That's worth two points.

After a touchdown or a field goal, the scoring team kicks off to the other team. After a safety, however, the team caught in its own end zone must kick the ball away to the scoring team from its own 20-yard line— either by kickoff or by a punt.

A receiver is about to catch a touchdown pass.

Positions, Everybody

Football plays might seem chaotic, but they actually are very organized. Each of the eleven players on a team has a role, and that role is usually determined by the position of the player.

On offense, there are five linemen: the center, who hikes the ball; the left and right guards to both sides of the center; and the left and right tackles outside the guards. They begin the play in a **three-point stance**, with one hand touching the ground. Their job is to drive the defensive linemen back.

The rest of the players handle the ball most of the time. For that reason, they're called *skill-position players*. The quarterback receives the ball from the center. He usually either hands it off to a running back or passes it to a receiver. The halfback and fullback are the running backs, lining up behind the quarterback. The wide receivers are the flanker and split end, who usually line up to the sides of the field. In addition, the tight end starts on the line next to the tackle and can either **block** or go out for a pass.

The quarterback is almost always the player who gets the play from the coach or who calls the play at the line of scrimmage. He is the field general, and calls the signals that let the center know when to hike the ball.

FOOTBALL FACTS

Football teams have eleven players. On offense, they include a center, two guards, and two tackles in the offensive line, then a tight end who functions as a blocker and receiver, two wide receivers, two running backs, and the quarterback. On defense, there are usually four down linemen and three linebackers (or the other way around), and four defensive backs.

The defense also has set plays and positions. In the 4–3 defense, there are four down linemen—two defensive tackles in the middle and one defensive end to each side—and three linebackers, one middle linebacker and one to each side. In the 3–4 defense, there are three down linemen—a nose guard on the center and two defensive ends and four linebackers, two in the middle and two to the outside. In both, there are four defensive backs: two cornerbacks to the outside and two safeties in the middle. In pass defense, a team can play either **man-to-man**, when each player covers an opponent, or **zone**, when each player covers an area.

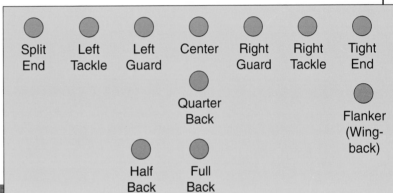

One common offensive formation is the winged T. In this formation, two running backs line up behind the quarterback. Another back, called the *flanker* or *wingback*, stands near the tight end.

Split End	Left Tackle	Left Guard	Center	Right Guard	Right Tackle	Tight End
			Quarter Back			Flanker (Wing-back)
		Half Back	Full Back			

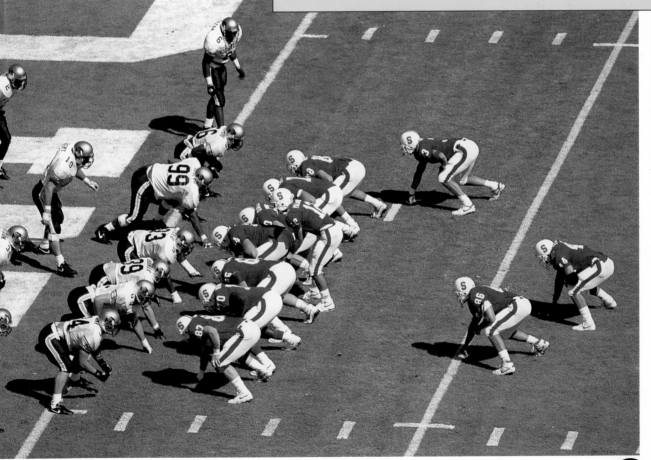

Suiting Up

With players running at each other at full speed and trying to knock each other to the ground, football can be a violent game. Equipment has developed over the years, however, to protect the players and make the game more safe.

From the earliest days, football players have worn shoulder pads and thigh guards. This is because most tackling is done with the shoulders, and in the best tackles the defensive player rams a shoulder into the ball carrier's, driving the legs out from under him or her. Football players sometimes wear elbow guards, especially on artificial turf, and knee pads usually are sewn into the pants. The jersey is made extra large in the shoulders, to fit over the pads and still tuck into the waist of the pants. Because quarterbacks sometimes have to stand in place to pass the ball, they are prone to especially hard tackles. So, they sometimes wear a protective vest around their midsection and under the jersey for extra protection.

Junior Seau, suited up for a game.

The football helmet has developed over the years from a high leather cap to a hard, molded-plastic hat with a face guard. Linemen usually wear extensive face guards, while quarterbacks and receivers usually wear face guards that allow them better vision. Whatever sort of helmet and face guard a player wears, and whatever position he plays, he must always remember that the helmet is for his protection and not to be used as a weapon—an illegal tactic known as spearing. Many football injuries, for both offensive and defensive players, are caused by a player trying to make a tackle with the helmet rather than with the arms and legs.

On grass fields, most football players wear shoes with cleats for better traction. On artificial turf, players usually switch to athletic shoes with ripple soles or other patterns on the bottom. In the 1934 NFL Championship game between the Chicago Bears and the New York Giants, the Giants won on a frozen field because they switched from cleats to plain old high-top gym shoes at half time.

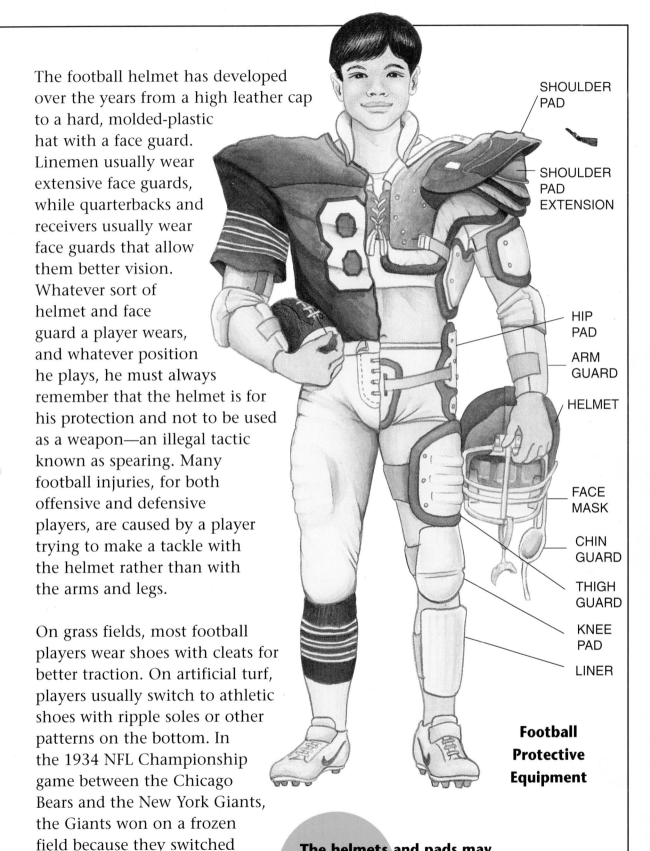

SHOULDER PAD

SHOULDER PAD EXTENSION

HIP PAD

ARM GUARD

HELMET

FACE MASK

CHIN GUARD

THIGH GUARD

KNEE PAD

LINER

Football Protective Equipment

The helmets and pads may look uncomfortable, but they are quite necessary.

Block and Tackle

Football has two unique skills no other sport has: blocking and tackling. It's said that the team that blocks and tackles best during a game will win.

Tackling is the main objective of the defense. What the defense tries to do is stop the ball carrier, keep the other team from getting a first down, and get the ball back to its offense through a punt. The key to that is good tackling.

Running backs are known for their strong legs and receivers are known for their speed. The best way to stop them is to come in low and cut their legs out from under them. But runners can fake tacklers, by shimmying their hips, for example. A runner's chest, however, is a relatively fixed target. So, the best tackle is made by aiming for the numbers on a runner's jersey, then sliding the helmet either to the left or right, wrapping the arms around the runner's midsection, and driving his legs out from under him. The best tackles are made with the shoulders and leg drive. A defender trying to tackle a runner high, by grabbing him around the shoulders, is almost sure to fail.

In pass blocking, an offensive lineman drops back and attempts to keep the pass rushers away from the quarterback.

The objective of the offense is to score, and to do that ball carriers must elude tackles. One of the keys to that is good blocking—keeping the defenders away from the ball carrier. Defenders can use their arms to grab and tackle the ball carrier, but offensive players cannot grab and tackle defenders. They must use their hands and arms to push defenders away without **holding** on. That is truly a skill.

The textbook tackle: shoulder into the ball carrier's midsection as the legs drive through.

All offensive players can block, but most blocking is done by the linemen in what's known as the **pit.** That's where the offense and defense line up face to face in three-point stances, with their hands to the ground. In blocking for a running play, offensive linemen drive forward low. In pass blocking, however, linemen stand up and drop back, forming a protective pocket around the quarterback. Most linemen would rather block for runs than passes, because they can be more aggressive, but both are important football skills.

FOOTBALL FACTS

Girls play football, too, although it becomes more difficult as boys and girls develop differently in high school. But girls are especially welcome in pee-wee and peanut leagues, and some areas form girls-only football leagues.

For run blocking, offensive linemen fire out, staying low on their opponents.

Hold It!

This may sound simple, but one of the basic tasks in football is to hold onto the ball once it's caught. When a runner drops the football, it's up for grabs. Whichever team gets the ball runs the next offensive play. In the standard football formation, play begins with the center hiking the football between his legs to the quarterback. The play begins with the ball pointed toward the end zones. But in hiking the ball, the center turns it sideways so that it fits right into the quarterback's two hands. From then on, it's always best to keep two hands on the ball.

When the quarterback hands the ball off to a running back, the runner usually tries to encircle it with his two arms and then cradle it in his midsection. Defenders try to strip the ball by tearing it out of a runner's hands, so carrying it with both arms around it offers the best protection.

Carrying the ball one-handed one tip is clutched in the hand, the other nestled into the crook of the elbow.

But a runner can't always be so cautious. Particularly in the open field, a runner runs best with one hand on the ball and both arms pumping in stride. The player can then use his or her free hand to fend off tacklers. The best way to carry the ball one-handed is to clutch the front tip of the ball with the hand, then tuck the back tip into the nook of the elbow, in the same way as you would carry a loaf of bread. That way, it's harder for a defensive player to get a hand on the end of the ball and tear it away.

Pointers

Receivers must have control of the ball before going out of bounds for a catch near the sideline to count. In the NFL, a receiver must get both feet down inbounds; in college and high school, a receiver must get one foot inbounds.

Terry Bradshaw prepares to hand off to Franco Harris, who is going to put two hands on the ball.

The Air War

Football can be beautiful when blockers open a path for a runner who darts right through. But for beauty, nothing can quite match a long passing play, when the quarterback throws and hits a receiver right in stride for a touchdown—a play known as a *bomb*.

Good quarterbacks make throwing a football look easy, but because of the funny shape of the ball, it's anything but. The most accurate pass and the easiest to catch is a spiral. In a spiral, the ball is rifled toward the target with spin to keep it on line. But this pass is far from easy.

A quarterback usually throws a football with the whole body, just as a baseball pitcher throws. He or she steps toward the target, and the shift in weight pulls the muscles across the stomach and chest to sling the arm forward. But a quarterback doesn't take a windup; the shorter the motion the better, with the ball going back behind the ear and then forward.

Troy Aikman flips a spiral to his receiver.

The proper grip for a quarterback: the two middle fingers rest across the seams of the laces, with the index finger a little away from the others for control.

When a center hikes the ball to a quarterback, it comes up sideways. That way, the ball fits right into the quarterback's hands. The tips of the two middle fingers of his throwing hand fit across the seams of the laces. The thumb, of course, grips the ball, and the pinkie steadies it. The index finger is forward, a little apart from the others, and the ball is thrown with a flick of the wrist, to add spin. When thrown well, the ball flows freely from the fingers right on line.

From there, of course, it's the receiver's job to catch it. The most common mistake receivers make is to try to run with the ball before it reaches them. A good receiver tries to stay in stride while watching the ball go into his hands. Then he tucks it away and runs with it.

Pointers

The defense usually rushes three or four down linemen. But the defense also can send any number of other players after the quarterback, a tactic known as the *blitz* or *red dog*. Most often coaches appoint the linebackers to blitz, but defensive backs can blitz in complex defensive schemes.

The Playbook

Football gets really interesting when each player performs his or her duty in a set play. There is almost no defense against a well-synchronized football team in which eleven players function as one. And the key to that is learning the plays in the playbook.

Vince Lombardi's power sweep, as designed on the blackboard or in the playbook: The guards pull out and the running back tries to get to the corner before the defensive linemen can chase him down.

Running backs don't just grab the ball and take off. They expect their linemen to block in certain ways to open holes in the line. The great coach Vince Lombardi called that "running to daylight." Lombardi mastered many exciting line plays to free his running backs. Maybe the most famous was the power sweep, in which the two guards pull out and run toward the side of the field. The other linemen try to block the defensive linemen, but even if one or two gets through, the running back is usually fast enough to get to the corner before they can. From there, the running back is behind two big linemen in the open field—plenty of daylight.

Pointers

A running back carrying the ball in one hand can use his free hand to fend off tacklers, a play known as a straight-arm. But the rules against holding or tackling a defensive player still apply. The runner can push a tackler away but not pull him down.

SE   LT   LG   C   RG   RT   TE

QB

HB   FB

FL

Pass plays are equally complex. With defensive backs trying to guard the receivers, quarterbacks usually call on the receivers to run set patterns. The quarterback and receiver know where the ball is going, but the defensive back does not. Sometimes a quarterback throws to a spot on the field before the receiver even makes his cut. When the receiver turns, there's the ball—almost impossible for a defender to break up.

The defense also has set plays. The two basic defensive formations are the 4–3 and the 3–4. In the 4–3, there are four down linemen and three linebackers behind them, and in the 3–4 there are three linemen and four linebackers. In both, there are four defensive backs. On passing downs, with long yardage to go for a first down, coaches frequently put in the "**nickel defense**," using five or more defensive backs. There are also two basic defensive schemes in pass coverage: the man-to-man and the zone. In man-to-man, each defensive player covers a certain receiver. In zone, each defender covers an area of the field.

Green Bay's Jerry Kramer clears the way for a Bart Starr touchdown during the 1967 Super Bowl.

Fouls and Flags

Football has referees who make sure both teams obey the rules. Most rules assure fair play. Blockers aren't allowed to hold on to defensive players. Defensive players are allowed to hold on to an offensive player only when they're tackling the ball carrier. That goes for defensive backs, who can be charged with **interference** if they try to tackle a receiver before he touches the ball. Likewise, if an offensive player moves or a defensive player crosses the line of scrimmage before the ball is snapped, that's **offside**.

Deion Sanders gets his hooks into a receiver a little before he ought to.

24

Other penalties try to protect the players from injuries. For instance, offensive players aren't allowed to block a defensive player from behind, especially below the waist, a penalty known as **clipping.** When an offensive player is down, or has run out of bounds, there is no need for extra defensive players to try to hit him—a penalty known as *piling on* or *unnecessary roughness.* No player may grab another player's face mask, which could snap a player's neck.

When an official detects a penalty, he throws a flag. If a play hasn't yet started, the penalty—usually assessed in yards either for the defense or the offense—is marched off right away. Otherwise, the play continues until the end. Then, the team that didn't commit the penalty has the choice of accepting the penalty, in which case the play doesn't count, or declining it, in which case the play stands. A team that scores a touchdown on a play where the defense was offside would certainly decline the penalty.

Some football penalties—such as clipping, or blocking from behind below the waist— are called to discourage injuries.

From Playgrounds to Stadiums

Kids play football on playgrounds and fields. But organized play usually begins for kids six years old to twelve years old in local pee-wee or peanut leagues. Those players might go on to the Pop Warner League, named after the great early college coach. But most players develop while performing for their high schools and colleges, and the very best go on to the professional leagues—the United States' National Football League (NFL) or the Canadian Football League.

Most high-school games are played on Friday nights or Saturday afternoons. High-school football is very serious, as any player will tell you, but most good high-school coaches stress the basics and team play. Winning or losing is less important than playing hard and playing together. Only a few of the best players on the average high-school team will receive football **scholarships** in college.

Through football, kids learn about teamwork.

American football is increasing in popularity in Europe. A popular British team is the Monarchs.

In college, the competition heats up. The pressure to win can be great at schools with storied histories, such as Notre Dame. But again, most of the players on a college team will not be playing on scholarships, but simply because they love the game and the camaraderie. On even the best teams, only a handful of players will go on to the pros. Many exceptional coaches prefer to remain at the college level because they like working with young men who enjoy the game as a sport rather than a career.

The NFL features the best football players in the world, and there, strategy is more important than ever. Most teams today look for players who are not only talented, but smart enough to handle the complexities of the pro game. The competition, both in games and for positions on a team, can be fierce. But the rewards can be great, both in money and in public acclaim.

FOOTBALL FACTS

In the NFL, various groups and publications give out Most Valuable Player or Player of the Year awards. In college, there is one prize above all: the Heisman Trophy, which goes to the best college football player in the nation. Ohio State running back Archie Griffin is the only player to win it twice.

The Greats

Football has changed much over the years, but a few greats establish themselves in every era.

One famous early player was Red Grange, "the Galloping Ghost," a running back who starred for the Chicago Bears. In the 1950s and '60s, Jim Brown set the standard for running backs, amassing 12,739 yards and scoring 126 touchdowns in only nine seasons. The Bears' great Walter Payton broke Brown's rushing record and holds it today with 16,726 yards. The San Francisco 49ers' wide receiver Jerry Rice broke Brown's record for touchdowns. Eric Dickerson took the record for most yards rushed in an NFL season in 1984, when he rushed 2,105 yards.

As for quarterbacks, Joe Montana is the highest-rated passer in NFL history, and he led his teams to four Super Bowl victories. Fran Tarkenton holds the record with 47,003 total passing yards, but Dan Marino broke his record of 342 touchdown passes and is gaining on Tarkenton in yardage. Other great quarterbacks include Johnny Unitas, Bart Starr, Terry Bradshaw, Steve Young, Troy Aikman, and John Elway.

Some defensive players and offensive linemen establish themselves as greats. Bronko Nagurski was a great running back for the Bears who later returned as a tackle. Other great linemen include Forrest Gregg, Mel Hein, Jim Ringo, Anthony Muñoz, and, on the other side of the ball, Deacon Jones, "Mean" Joe Green, Alan Page, Merlin Olsen, and Reggie White. Linebackers Dick Butkus and Lawrence Taylor and defensive back Ronnie Lott are among the best and toughest football players of all time.

Steve Young exults after another hard-earned victory.

There have been great coaches both in the colleges and the pros. Great college coaches include Notre Dame's Knute Rockne, Alabama's "Bear" Bryant, and, more recently, Penn State's Joe Paterno.

In the pros, the Bears' George Halas helped organize the NFL and went on to win 324 games, a record that stood until Don Shula recently broke it. Other great NFL coaches include Vince Lombardi, Paul Brown, John Madden, and Bill Walsh.

The Pro Football Hall of Fame in Canton, Ohio, the birthplace of the NFL.

Glossary

block When offensive players attempt to protect the ball carrier from defensive players; hands may be used, but not to grab or hold the defensive players.

clipping Blocking a player from behind, usually below the waist.

end zone Area beyond the goal line, where touchdowns are scored.

extra point or point after touchdown (PAT) The kick performed from a spot on the 3-yard line after a touchdown is scored; good for one point.

field goal Kick from the field through the uprights; good for three points.

fumble When an offensive player drops the ball; ball is live and whichever team recovers it goes on offense.

goal posts Designate the area, 18½ feet wide and 10 yards off the grounds, where kicks must go to be called good.

hash marks The marks near the center of the field that show the referees where to spot the football when it has been run out of bounds or to the sides of the field.

hike The center's act of starting the play, sending the ball to the quarterback, punter, or field-goal holder.

holding When an offensive or defensive player illegally grabs an opposing player.

incomplete When a pass play is not caught by a receiver or defender; ball returns to original line of scrimmage.

interception When a defensive player catches a pass intended for an offensive receiver.

interference When a receiver or defender interferes with the opponent's fair chance to catch or intercept a pass.

kickoff The play at the start of a game, or after a touchdown and extra point, in which a team kicks the ball to the other team.

line of scrimmage The yard line where a play starts.

man-to-man coverage Defensive scheme where every player covers a man on the other team.

National Football League The world's major professional football league, organized in 1920. The rival American Football League was formed in 1960. They merged into the American and National Conferences of the NFL in 1970.

nickel defense A defense where a coach inserts a fifth defensive back in a passing situation.

offside When a player crosses the line of scrimmage before the play begins.

pass Ball thrown forward from behind the line of scrimmage.

pigskin An old term for a football, even though most official footballs are now made from leather.

pit The line where offensive and defensive linemen face off.

playbook The array of plays and defenses a team has.

punting The act of kicking away the football in midair when dropped from the hands; a defensive maneuver performed by the offense, usually on the fourth down.

safety When the defensive team traps the offense in its own end zone; good for two points.

scholarship When talented players attend college for free or at a reduced fee in exchange for playing on the football team.

sidelines Areas to the sides of field, out of bounds; where the team members not on the field gather.

tackle When a defensive player drags down the offensive ball carrier or pushes him out of bounds; play ends, next play begins at same spot.

three-point stance The stance linemen assume, referring to feet and one hand on the ground, that permits them to start the play driving forward and low to the ground.

touchdown Running or catching a ball in the end zone; good for six points.

zone An area of the field, or a defensive scheme where players are assigned an area to cover.

Index